Birth of
an Island

By MILLICENT E. SELSAM

Illustrated by WINIFRED LUBELL

SCHOLASTIC BOOK SERVICES
NEW YORK • TORONTO • LONDON • AUCKLAND • SYDNEY • TOKYO

Other books by Millicent E. Selsam and Winifred Lubell:

SEE THROUGH THE FOREST

SEE THROUGH THE JUNGLE

SEE THROUGH THE SEA

SEE THROUGH THE LAKE

Text copyright© 1959 by Millicent E. Selsam. Pictures copyright© 1959 by Winnifred Lubell. This edition is published by Scholastic Book Services, a division of Scholastic Magazines, Inc., by arrangement with Harper & Row, Publishers.

22 21 20 19 18 17 16 15   8 9/7 0/8

About this book

Every now and then new islands appear in the sea. They are formed in different ways. But most ocean islands are formed when undersea volcanoes erupt and pile up masses of rock.

No matter how an island forms, plants and animals soon come to the island. Scientists had a wonderful opportunity to study how this happens when the volcano on the island of Krakatoa, near Java, blew up in 1883. Most of the island was destroyed. A small part remained, and this was covered with a deep layer of hot lava and burning ashes. Here was a new island with no living thing on it. At intervals through the years that followed, the scientists went to the island to see what had happened.

This book is based on their studies. Even though it tells the story of a tropical island surrounded by warm seas, the way in which the plants and animals come to it is typical of the way plants and animals have come to any island.

ONCE upon a time, far off in the middle of a big ocean, miles from the nearest land, a crack opened in an undersea volcano. With a rumble and a roar, an explosion of red-hot lava and burning ashes burst forth. Huge black clouds swirled to the sky. The water boiled, and white steam mixed with the fiery cloud.

The hot lava piled higher and higher, and spread wider and wider. In this way, slowly, an island rose up in the sea.

The hot lava cooled and stiffened into shining black rock. Hot sun beat down on the rock. Cool rains fell. Now hot, now cold, the rock split and gradually broke to pieces. In the course of time, a fine crumbly soil covered the island. Where the rock met the sea, waves dashed against it, tore away pieces, and ground them to sand.

Nothing lived on the naked soil. Not as yet. But slowly, through the years, the island became covered with green plants. And slowly, animals began to move over its beaches and hills. How did they get there?

Around the island the wind roared, the ocean crashed, and the birds flapped their wings. The wind, the sea, and the birds were at work bringing life to the new island.

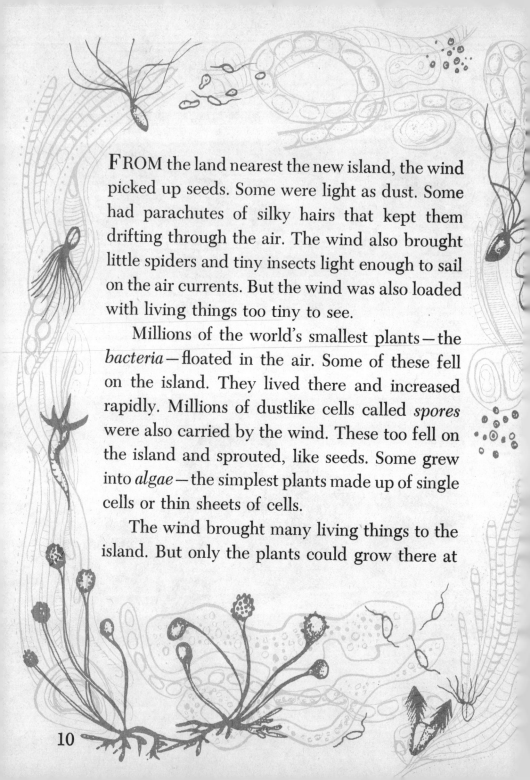

FROM the land nearest the new island, the wind picked up seeds. Some were light as dust. Some had parachutes of silky hairs that kept them drifting through the air. The wind also brought little spiders and tiny insects light enough to sail on the air currents. But the wind was also loaded with living things too tiny to see.

Millions of the world's smallest plants—the *bacteria*—floated in the air. Some of these fell on the island. They lived there and increased rapidly. Millions of dustlike cells called *spores* were also carried by the wind. These too fell on the island and sprouted, like seeds. Some grew into *algae*—the simplest plants made up of single cells or thin sheets of cells.

The wind brought many living things to the island. But only the plants could grow there at

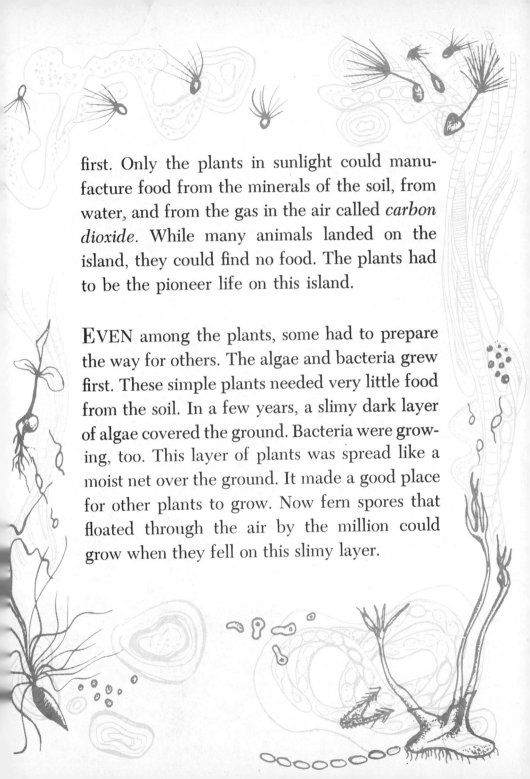

first. Only the plants in sunlight could manufacture food from the minerals of the soil, from water, and from the gas in the air called *carbon dioxide*. While many animals landed on the island, they could find no food. The plants had to be the pioneer life on this island.

EVEN among the plants, some had to prepare the way for others. The algae and bacteria grew first. These simple plants needed very little food from the soil. In a few years, a slimy dark layer of algae covered the ground. Bacteria were growing, too. This layer of plants was spread like a moist net over the ground. It made a good place for other plants to grow. Now fern spores that floated through the air by the million could grow when they fell on this slimy layer.

All this time, some of the algae and ferns were dying and decaying. This dead plant material, called *humus*, made the soil spongy. Now the soil could hold air and water better. Besides, the humus was a storehouse of minerals and other chemicals. Slowly the soil became richer. At last other plants that needed more fertile ground could grow. The light dustlike seeds, the seeds with parachutes of silky hairs, and the light grains of grasses now could sprout. Soon the hills were covered with grasses and other plants.

All these plants were growing in the inland slopes and hills. There the higher land stopped the wind and forced it to drop its load of seeds and spores. But down on the beach, the ocean was rolling in, bringing the flotsam and jetsam of the sea.

The sea tossed onto the shore tree stems, broken branches, seaweeds, and hundreds of seeds and fruits. Coconuts, the nuts of other palms, and the fruits of tropical shore plants were piled along the beach. Some of the fruits and seeds looked as fresh as if they had just fallen from the tree. They came from the nearest islands. Others showed the rubbings and scratchings of a long journey. But all of them could float and ride the waves like tiny boats.

The coconuts on the beach had light husks full of air spaces that made wonderful life jackets for the coconut seeds inside. The tough inner wall of the fruit protected the seed from the sea water. No wonder the coconut palm has spread to the shores of nearly every tropical island.

THE other fruits and seeds on the shore were suited to sea travel in much the same way. Such seeds and fruits have traveled far and wide over the waters of the earth. That is why, all around the world, the shore plants of islands and coasts in the tropical seas are very much the same.

Wherever the heaps on the beach were piled high, there was moisture and humus in which the sea-borne seeds could sprout.

A band of fresh green soon moved in from the shore of the island.

While this green mantle was spreading over the island, the animals kept arriving. They came by wind, by sea, and on their own wings.

Beetles, mosquitoes, moths, and butterflies flew over from the nearest islands, or were carried by the wind. When a shower of dragonflies fell on the island one day, some stayed and fed on the smaller insects they found there.

Big palm leaves, blown like kites through the sky, carried tiny animal passengers. Ants and little land snails arrived in this way.

Large bats flew over on strong wings.

17

Down on the shore, the sea kept bringing in animal passengers who rode the waves on bits of wood or shells or on rafts of trees and logs.

One day, it was a little gecko lizard that came riding in on top of a coconut shell.

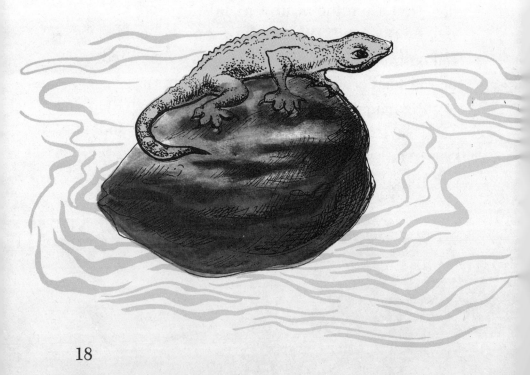

Another day, a whole family of skink lizards came in on a tree torn up by its roots in a tropical gale.

A large python snake came ashore wrapped
around the trunk of a floating fig tree.

A raft of trees jammed together floated in.
It had many animal passengers. One of the logs
was honeycombed with tunnels that were the

home of hundreds of wood-boring beetles. In the tunnels were the eggs, the young, and many adult beetles.

On the same raft there was a tiny spider. It had a sac of eggs attached to its body. When they hatched, the island had a whole colony of spiders.

In the earth jammed between two logs were several earthworms, a colony of ants, and lots of eggs of land snails.

Time after time, the sea brought such new animal colonists to the island.

At first, there had been nothing for them to eat on the barren island except the plant scraps thrown up on the shore. But now the animals that fed on plants could find food and could live on the island. There were leaves to munch, stems and roots to bite, seeds to swallow, the nectar of flowers to sip, and the juice of leaves to suck. Now too, other animals that preyed on the plant eaters could live on the island. A spider, for example, found plenty of insects to eat, for the insects now had a world of green plants to feed on.

Birds flew to the island all the time. In the beginning, most of them were sea birds that stopped on the island to rest. At first the naked island did not attract land birds, because there was no shade and little food. But as the island turned green, they too stopped, and some stayed.

Golden orioles, little black and crimson flower-peckers, and thrushes ate insects or the grains of grasses, or sucked the juice of flowers.

ALL the birds helped to bring more plants to the island—the birds that visited and the ones that stayed. A flock of sea birds—petrels—stayed on the island for only a little while. But they had just left their nesting grounds on another island. On their feathers and bills, and tucked away in cracks between their claws, were seeds from the thick matting of plants where they had nested. These new seeds sprouted and grew on the island.

One beautiful island morning, hundreds of fruit pigeons came. At sunrise that day, they had been on a nearby island feeding on the small black fruits of fig trees. The pulpy fruits they had swallowed were digested, but the seeds passed right through their digestive tracts and dropped out on the ground.

And so fig trees came to the new island.

ALWAYS the birds and the wind and the sea were bringing new seeds to the island. And so the island changed still more. The grassy plains shrank, and small patches of trees merged into forests. Slowly, the forest green spread down the slopes of the hills and up from the shore.

As the trees grew, leaves kept falling from the branches, adding a thick layer of leaf humus to the forest soil. More and more birds came to eat the seeds and fruits of the trees. And each time they dropped the seeds of new trees to sprout in the rich soil.

The trees threw long shadows on the ground. Moisture rose from soil and plants, and lingered in the forest. Now the plants that could grow only in damp, shady places took root.

Climbing plants wound their way up through the trees. Other plants took root in the moist crannies of the forest trees, and there were orchids, roses, and lovely pineapple-like plants.

One day a steamship anchored off the island. Several rowboats were launched and made their way to shore. In the boats were some scientists who had come to the island to study its animals. Each day, for a week, they left the steamship and came to the island to count the animals. By the time they went away they had added something new to the life of the island: several rats.

These stowaways, hidden on the ship, came ashore in some packing cases the scientists brought with them for their work. Besides the bats, which had flown there, these rats were the only other *mammals* on the island. (Mammals are warm-blooded, hairy animals that suckle their young.)

Here is the count of the different *species* or kinds of animals that the scientists found on this island thirty-eight years after it had risen in the sea:

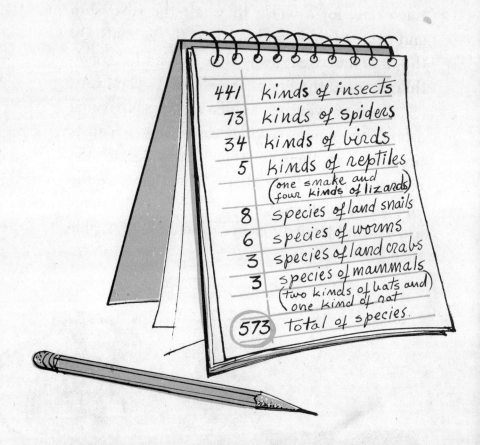

441	kinds of insects
73	kinds of spiders
34	kinds of birds
5	kinds of reptiles (one snake and four kinds of lizards)
8	species of land snails
6	species of worms
3	species of land crabs
3	species of mammals (two kinds of bats and one kind of rat)
573	Total of species.

Look this list over carefully. It shows something important about living things on all ocean islands.

Most of the species are animals that could either have flown to the island or been blown there by the wind. These are the insects, spiders, birds, and bats.

Now think about what's missing from this list. Where are the frogs or toads or salamanders or fresh-water fish? There simply aren't any. These animals and their eggs would probably be injured by a long journey over sea water, even on a raft.

And what about mammals? Only three kinds live on the island: a rat and two species of bats. Compare this with the huge number of mammals you can find on any continent! The island has none of the mammals we know — the bears, skunks, raccoons, squirrels, elephants, beavers, lions, tigers, horses, deer, or others you can name. These animals cannot fly or swim across the sea, and most of them are too big to come over on rafts.

OVER a hundred years ago Charles Darwin, the famous naturalist, made a trip around the world on the ship *Beagle*. He stopped at many tropical islands and kept track of the species of animals he saw. He pointed out the very same facts that our list shows. Islands in the ocean usually have no fresh-water animals and very few mammals.

Now let's take a trip into the future to see our island again many thousands of years after it first rose in the sea. If we look with the eyes of a scientist, we will see some remarkable things. Here on the island are some new birds, new reptiles, new insects, new plants that do not exist on any other island or continent in the world. They look like the earlier ones we saw coming to this island, but they are strangely different in many ways.

ALL over the earth during these thousands of years, animals and plants have been changing, just as they changed all through the past history of the earth. Everywhere new types have arisen, old types have died out, and some have stayed pretty much the same. Of course, this has happened on continents as well as on the islands. But ocean islands are a bit different.

The stragglers that come to the island find themselves *separated from the rest of their kind* and can no longer mate with them as they do on continents.

Suppose a female swallow comes to the island with feathers more purple than blue, even though all the other members of her species have blue feathers. She builds a nest and lays some eggs. Among the new little birds that hatch from these eggs, a few have purple feathers — some even more purple than the mother bird's. These birds grow up, mate, and lay more eggs. Gradually, over the years, more and more of the great-grandchildren and great-great-great-grandchildren of this one little bird have purple feathers, until now there is a purple swallow which is found only on this island. On the mainland from which the mother swallow came, this purpleness may have disappeared as the newly hatched swallows grew up and mated with the bluer members of their kind.

Or suppose that on our island some wingless flies appear in a group of ordinary flies with wings. These wingless flies survive because they have plenty of flower nectar for food, and because they may have no enemies on the island from which they have to escape by flying. On the mainland, this same type of fly may have been wiped out. Flies without wings may have another advantage on the island. When strong gales blow, as they often do, many of the winged insects flying in the air are carried off over the ocean, while the wingless ones stay to have more young like themselves.

And so the life on our island goes on in its own special way.

ISLANDS may rise in the ocean and then sink back into the water and disappear. This has happened countless times. But when islands do remain, they change. Bare rock slowly changes to soil. Sea currents toss seeds and driftwood carrying animal passengers onto the shore. The wind brings spores, seeds, insects, and birds from the land nearest the new island.

The plant world prepares the way for the animal world. And in both worlds, some plants and animals prepare the way for others. Slowly, the island is changed from bare rock to green forests alive with animals. And thousands of years after it first rose in the sea, the ocean island will have new kinds of animals and plants that are not found anywhere else on earth.

A note from the author

Islands appear in the most unexpected places! In 1958 the Army Engineers dredged the channel in Great South Bay which lies between Long Island and Fire Island, N. Y. They poured the dredged sand onto a shallow area nearby, and an island was born.

When I saw this new island, I wondered how long it would take for plants and animals to get there. In 1958 there was nothing on the island but the sand and shells dredged from the bottom of the bay. The next year I counted about 19 different kinds of plants growing on it. This started me on a search for a scientist who would study the island in succeeding years. Finally Dr.

Jack McCormick, then with the American Museum of Natural History, and now at Ohio State University, agreed to do such a study. In October, 1959, he collected 34 plants and identified them. In 1960 he returned to find 69 species of plants. In 1961 there were 74 species, but 21 of them were new to the island and 16 kinds that had been there in 1960 had disappeared. By 1962 green vegetation covered almost three quarters of the island.

Having read this book, you probably know how these plants got there. But if you did not know, and you had a chance to sit on this island, you would soon find the answer anyway. You hear the wind blow, and you can imagine the thousands of light seeds it must carry. You watch the waves lap the shore and realize that many seeds must have floated to the island. Then the birds scream overhead, and you think of the many seeds they carry on their feet, and in their bills and feathers. And you know that many seeds they may have swallowed elsewhere have passed out with their droppings onto this new island.

The animal population so far is limited to insects and birds. The only mammals are people who visit the island in their boats to picnic. This little island is a pleasant spot, but it is also a miniature exhibit of the way plants and animals come to islands all over the world.

Look for a new island yourself.

Millicent E. Selsam